Raspberry Sauce Cookbook

Delicious Recipes and Creative Uses for Raspberry Sauces

While every precaution has been taken in the preparation of this book, the publisher assumes no responsibility for errors or omissions, or for damages resulting from the use of the information contained herein.

RASPBERRY SAUCE COOKBOOK

First edition. December 1, 2023.

ISBN: 979-8223169048

Written by john ahmad.

Table of Contents

John Ahmad

Chapter 1: Introduction to Raspberry Sauces

Raspberry sauces are a delightful addition to any culinary repertoire. Bursting with vibrant color and a sweet-tart flavor profile, these sauces can transform ordinary dishes into extraordinary creations. In this chapter, we will embark on a journey to discover the world of raspberry sauces, from their humble beginnings to their versatile applications in a wide range of dishes.

What Are Raspberry Sauces?

Raspberry sauces are a type of fruit-based sauce made primarily from raspberries. They are known for their bright red or pink hue, which adds a burst of color to any dish. The main ingredient, raspberries, are not only visually appealing but also packed with vitamins, antioxidants, and a delightful natural sweetness.

Raspberry sauces can vary in texture and sweetness, depending on how they are prepared. Some are smooth and pourable, while others may have a thicker, chunkier consistency. Their sweetness can be adjusted to suit your taste, making them a versatile addition to both sweet and savory dishes.

The Versatility of Raspberry Sauces

One of the remarkable qualities of raspberry sauces is their incredible versatility. While they are often associated with desserts, they can be used in a wide range of culinary creations, including breakfast, lunch, dinner, and even beverages. Here are some of the many ways you can use raspberry sauces:

Desserts: Raspberry sauces are a classic accompaniment for desserts like ice cream, cheesecake, and chocolate fondue. They can also be used as a drizzle over pastries and cakes.

Breakfast: Start your day with a burst of raspberry flavor by adding raspberry sauce to pancakes, waffles, yogurt parfaits, or drizzling it over your morning oatmeal.

Savory Dishes: Raspberry sauces can be used in savory applications, such as glazes for grilled meats, salad dressings, or as a dipping sauce for appetizers.

Beverages: Raspberry sauce can elevate your drink game. Use it in cocktails, mocktails, smoothies, and even homemade fruit sodas.

Special Occasions: Raspberry sauces can make any celebration more special. Whether it's a wedding cake, champagne sauce for toasts, or a romantic fondue night, raspberries bring elegance and flavor.

How to Make the Perfect Raspberry Sauce

Making raspberry sauce is a straightforward process that allows you to control the sweetness and texture to suit your preferences. Here's a basic recipe to get you started:

Ingredients:

- 2 cups fresh raspberries (or frozen, thawed)
- 1/2 cup granulated sugar (adjust to taste)
- 1 tablespoon lemon juice (freshly squeezed)

Instructions:

1. Prepare the Raspberries: If using fresh raspberries, rinse them gently and pat them dry. If using frozen raspberries, allow them to thaw.
2. Combine Ingredients: In a saucepan, combine the raspberries, sugar, and lemon juice. The lemon juice enhances the raspberry flavor and helps balance the sweetness.
3. Cook: Over medium heat, bring the mixture to a gentle simmer while stirring occasionally. Continue simmering for about 5-7 minutes, or until the raspberries break down and the sauce thickens.
4. Strain (Optional): If you prefer a smoother sauce without seeds, you can strain the sauce through a fine-mesh sieve to remove the seeds. Press the sauce through the sieve using a spatula.
5. Cool and Store: Allow the raspberry sauce to cool to room temperature. It will continue to thicken as it cools. Once cooled, transfer it to an airtight container and refrigerate. Raspberry sauce can be stored in the refrigerator for up to two weeks.

Now that you've been introduced to the world of raspberry sauces and know how to make a basic raspberry sauce, you're ready to explore the delicious recipes and creative uses for raspberry sauces in the upcoming chapters. Whether you're a seasoned cook or a novice in the kitchen, there's something in this cookbook for everyone. So, let's dive in and discover the culinary wonders that raspberry sauces have to offer.

Chapter 2: Classic Raspberry Sauce Recipes

In this chapter, we'll explore three classic raspberry sauce recipes that are essential in any kitchen. These recipes will serve as a foundation for your raspberry sauce adventures, whether you're looking for a simple topping for your morning pancakes or a flavorful filling for desserts.

Recipe 1: Basic Raspberry Coulis
Ingredients:

- 2 cups fresh raspberries (or frozen, thawed)
- 1/2 cup granulated sugar (adjust to taste)
- 1 tablespoon lemon juice (freshly squeezed)

Instructions:

1. Prepare the Raspberries: Rinse the raspberries gently if using fresh ones. Pat them dry. If using frozen raspberries, make sure they are thawed.
2. Combine Ingredients: In a saucepan, combine the raspberries, sugar, and lemon juice. The lemon juice enhances the raspberry flavor and balances the sweetness.
3. Cook: Over medium heat, bring the mixture to a gentle simmer while stirring occasionally. Continue simmering for about 5-7 minutes, or until the raspberries break down and the sauce thickens.
4. Strain (Optional): If you prefer a smoother sauce without seeds, strain the sauce through a fine-mesh sieve to remove the seeds. Press the sauce through the sieve using a spatula.
5. Cool and Store: Allow the raspberry coulis to cool to room temperature. It will thicken further as it cools. Once cooled, transfer it to an airtight container and refrigerate. Raspberry

coulis can be stored in the refrigerator for up to two weeks.

6. Usage: Raspberry coulis is a versatile sauce that can be used to garnish desserts like cheesecake, panna cotta, or ice cream. It's also a fantastic drizzle for fresh fruit salads or a sweet addition to breakfast dishes.

Recipe 2: Raspberry Jam
Ingredients:

- 4 cups fresh raspberries (or frozen, thawed)
- 4 cups granulated sugar
- 1/4 cup lemon juice (freshly squeezed)

Instructions:

1. Prepare the Raspberries: Rinse the raspberries gently if using fresh ones. Pat them dry. If using frozen raspberries, make sure they are thawed.
2. Combine Ingredients: In a large, heavy-bottomed pot, combine the raspberries, sugar, and lemon juice. Stir well to combine.
3. Cook: Over medium-high heat, bring the mixture to a boil, stirring frequently. Once it boils, reduce the heat to medium-low and simmer for about 20-25 minutes, or until the jam thickens and reaches the desired consistency. Skim off any foam that forms on the surface.
4. Test for Doneness: To check if the jam is ready, place a small amount on a cold plate. If it wrinkles and holds its shape when you push it with your finger, it's done.
5. Cool and Store: Allow the raspberry jam to cool for a few minutes, then transfer it to clean, sterilized jars. Seal the jars while the jam is still hot. Once cooled, store the jam in a cool, dark place. It can be stored for up to a year.
6. Usage: Raspberry jam is a beloved classic for spreading on toast,

muffins, and scones. It's also a fantastic filling for thumbprint cookies, pastries, and layer cakes.

Recipe 3: Raspberry Drizzle for Desserts
Ingredients:

- 1/2 cup fresh raspberries (or frozen, thawed)
- 1/4 cup confectioners' sugar
- 1 tablespoon lemon juice (freshly squeezed)

Instructions:
Prepare the Raspberries: Rinse the raspberries gently if using fresh ones. Pat them dry. If using frozen raspberries, make sure they are thawed.

Combine Ingredients: In a blender or food processor, combine the raspberries, confectioners' sugar, and lemon juice. Blend until smooth.

Strain (Optional): If you prefer a smoother drizzle without seeds, strain the mixture through a fine-mesh sieve to remove the seeds.

Serve: This raspberry drizzle is best served immediately over desserts like cheesecake, chocolate mousse, or vanilla ice cream. You can also store it in the refrigerator for a day or two, but it's at its freshest when served immediately.

These classic raspberry sauce recipes are the building blocks for adding a burst of raspberry flavor to your culinary creations. In the upcoming chapters, we'll explore more specialized uses for raspberry sauces, from breakfast delights to savory dishes and sweet treats. Get ready to elevate your cooking and impress your guests with the versatility and deliciousness of raspberry sauces.

Chapter 3: Breakfast Delights with Raspberry Sauce

Breakfast is the most important meal of the day, and what better way to start it than with the vibrant flavors of raspberry sauce? In this chapter, we'll explore three breakfast recipes that incorporate raspberry sauce to elevate your morning dining experience.

Recipe 1: Raspberry Pancakes

Ingredients:

- 1 cup all-purpose flour
- 2 tablespoons granulated sugar
- 1 teaspoon baking powder
- 1/2 teaspoon baking soda
- 1/4 teaspoon salt
- 1 cup buttermilk
- 1 large egg
- 2 tablespoons unsalted butter, melted
- 1/2 cup fresh raspberries
- Raspberry sauce (for drizzling)

Instructions:

1. Prepare the Batter: In a mixing bowl, whisk together the flour, sugar, baking powder, baking soda, and salt.
2. Combine Wet Ingredients: In another bowl, whisk together the buttermilk, egg, and melted butter.
3. Mix Dry and Wet Ingredients: Pour the wet ingredients into the dry ingredients and stir until just combined. Be careful not to overmix; a few lumps are okay.
4. Add Raspberries: Gently fold in the fresh raspberries into the batter.

5. Cook Pancakes: Heat a non-stick skillet or griddle over medium heat and lightly grease it with butter or cooking spray. Pour 1/4 cup of batter for each pancake onto the skillet. Cook until bubbles form on the surface, then flip and cook until golden brown on both sides.

6. Serve: Stack the pancakes on a plate and drizzle generously with raspberry sauce. Serve warm.

Recipe 2: Yogurt Parfait with Raspberry Swirl
Ingredients:

- 1 cup Greek yogurt
- 1/2 cup granola
- 1/2 cup fresh raspberries
- 2 tablespoons honey
- Raspberry sauce (for swirling)

Instructions:

1. Layer Yogurt and Granola: In a serving glass or bowl, start by layering half of the Greek yogurt.
2. Add Granola: Sprinkle half of the granola over the yogurt layer.
3. Add Raspberries: Add half of the fresh raspberries.
4. Drizzle Honey: Drizzle 1 tablespoon of honey over the raspberries.
5. Repeat Layers: Repeat the layers with the remaining yogurt, granola, raspberries, and honey.
6. Swirl with Raspberry Sauce: Finish the parfait by drizzling raspberry sauce over the top. Use a skewer or spoon to gently swirl the sauce into the yogurt.
7. Serve: Serve immediately for a delightful and healthy breakfast.

Recipe 3: Raspberry-Filled Crepes
Ingredients:
For the Crepes:

- 1 cup all-purpose flour
- 2 large eggs
- 1 1/4 cups milk
- 2 tablespoons unsalted butter, melted
- 1/4 teaspoon salt

For the Filling:

- 1 cup fresh raspberries
- 1/4 cup raspberry sauce
- Confectioners' sugar (for dusting)

Instructions:
For the Crepes:
Prepare the Batter: In a blender, combine the flour, eggs, milk, melted butter, and salt. Blend until smooth. Let the batter rest for 15-20 minutes.

Cook the Crepes: Heat a non-stick skillet over medium-high heat and lightly grease it with butter or cooking spray. Pour 1/4 cup of batter into the skillet, swirling it to coat the bottom evenly. Cook for about 1-2 minutes per side, or until lightly golden. Repeat with the remaining batter, stacking the crepes on a plate.

For the Filling:
Assemble the Crepes: Place a crepe on a serving plate. Spread a spoonful of raspberry sauce over the crepe, then scatter fresh raspberries over the sauce.

Fold and Serve: Fold the crepe in half, then in half again to form a triangle. Dust with confectioners' sugar and drizzle with a bit more raspberry sauce. Serve warm.

These breakfast delights with raspberry sauce are sure to brighten your morning and kickstart your day with a burst of flavor. In the following chapters, we'll continue exploring the versatility of raspberry sauces in various culinary creations. Enjoy your delicious raspberry-infused breakfast!

Chapter 4: Sweet Treats with Raspberry Sauce

Indulge your sweet tooth with the delectable recipes in this chapter. Raspberry sauce adds a burst of flavor and a touch of elegance to these sweet treats, making them perfect for special occasions or simply satisfying your dessert cravings.

Recipe 1: Raspberry Swirl Cheesecake

Ingredients:

For the Crust:

- 1 1/2 cups graham cracker crumbs
- 1/4 cup granulated sugar
- 1/2 cup unsalted butter, melted

For the Cheesecake Filling:

- 3 (8-ounce) packages cream cheese, softened
- 1 cup granulated sugar
- 3 large eggs
- 1 teaspoon vanilla extract

For the Raspberry Swirl:

- 1/2 cup raspberry sauce

Instructions:

For the Crust:

Prepare the Crust: In a mixing bowl, combine the graham cracker crumbs, sugar, and melted butter. Press the mixture into the bottom of a 9-inch springform pan to create an even crust.

For the Cheesecake Filling:

Preheat Oven: Preheat your oven to 325°F (160°C).

Prepare Cheesecake Filling: In a large mixing bowl, beat the softened cream cheese until smooth. Gradually add the sugar, eggs, and vanilla extract, and continue to beat until well combined.

Pour Cheesecake Filling: Pour the cheesecake filling over the prepared crust in the springform pan.

For the Raspberry Swirl:

Add Raspberry Sauce: Spoon dollops of raspberry sauce onto the surface of the cheesecake filling.

Swirl: Use a knife or a skewer to gently swirl the raspberry sauce into the cheesecake filling, creating a marbled effect.

Bake: Bake the cheesecake in the preheated oven for 45-50 minutes or until the edges are set, and the center is slightly jiggly.

Cool and Chill: Allow the cheesecake to cool to room temperature in the oven with the door ajar. Once cooled, refrigerate for at least 4 hours or overnight.

Serve: Drizzle additional raspberry sauce over individual slices before serving.

Recipe 2: Chocolate Raspberry Tart

Ingredients:

For the Chocolate Crust:

- 1 1/4 cups all-purpose flour
- 1/4 cup unsweetened cocoa powder
- 1/4 cup granulated sugar
- 1/2 cup unsalted butter, cold and cubed

For the Chocolate Ganache:

- 1 cup semisweet chocolate chips
- 1/2 cup heavy cream

For the Raspberry Filling:

- 1 cup fresh raspberries
- 1/4 cup raspberry sauce
- Fresh raspberries and mint leaves for garnish

Instructions:
For the Chocolate Crust:
Prepare the Crust: In a food processor, combine the flour, cocoa powder, and sugar. Add the cold, cubed butter and pulse until the mixture resembles coarse crumbs.

Form the Dough: Turn the mixture out onto a lightly floured surface and knead it together to form a dough. Press the dough into a 9-inch tart pan with a removable bottom, making sure to cover the bottom and sides evenly. Chill the crust in the refrigerator for 30 minutes.

Preheat Oven: Preheat your oven to 350°F (175°C).

Bake the Crust: Bake the chocolate crust in the preheated oven for 15-18 minutes or until it's set. Allow it to cool completely.

For the Chocolate Ganache:
Prepare the Ganache: Place the semisweet chocolate chips in a heatproof bowl. In a small saucepan, heat the heavy cream over medium-low heat until it simmers. Pour the hot cream over the chocolate chips and let it sit for a minute. Stir until smooth and glossy.

For the Raspberry Filling:
Assemble the Tart: Spread the raspberry sauce over the cooled chocolate crust. Arrange fresh raspberries on top.

Pour the Ganache: Pour the chocolate ganache over the raspberries, ensuring an even layer.

Chill: Refrigerate the tart for at least 2 hours or until the ganache is set.

Garnish: Before serving, garnish with additional fresh raspberries and mint leaves.

Recipe 3: Raspberry Ice Cream
Ingredients:

- 2 cups heavy cream
- 1 cup whole milk
- 3/4 cup granulated sugar
- 1 teaspoon vanilla extract
- 1 cup fresh raspberries
- 1/2 cup raspberry sauce

Instructions:

Prepare the Ice Cream Base: In a mixing bowl, whisk together the heavy cream, whole milk, sugar, and vanilla extract until the sugar is completely dissolved.

Blend Raspberries: In a blender, puree the fresh raspberries until smooth. If desired, strain the puree through a fine-mesh sieve to remove the seeds.

Combine Raspberry Puree: Stir the raspberry puree into the ice cream base until well combined.

Churn: Pour the mixture into an ice cream maker and churn according to the manufacturer's instructions.

Swirl with Raspberry Sauce: When the ice cream is almost done churning, drizzle in the raspberry sauce. Churn for a few more seconds to create a swirl effect.

Freeze: Transfer the raspberry ice cream to an airtight container and freeze for a few hours or until firm.

Serve: Scoop and serve your homemade raspberry ice cream in bowls or cones.

These sweet treats with raspberry sauce are perfect for satisfying your dessert cravings or impressing guests with your culinary skills. Continue exploring the world of raspberry sauces in the following chapters for even more delightful creations. Enjoy these irresistible desserts!

Chapter 5: Savory Raspberry Sauce Creations

Raspberry sauce isn't just for sweet dishes; it also shines in savory creations, adding a delightful balance of sweet and tart flavors to your favorite savory recipes. In this chapter, we'll explore three savory raspberry sauce recipes that will elevate your culinary game.

Recipe 1: Raspberry Balsamic Glaze

Ingredients:

- 1 cup fresh raspberries
- 1/2 cup balsamic vinegar
- 1/4 cup granulated sugar
- 1 teaspoon Dijon mustard
- Salt and pepper to taste

Instructions:

1. Combine Ingredients: In a saucepan, combine the fresh raspberries, balsamic vinegar, and granulated sugar. Bring to a gentle simmer over medium heat.
2. Simmer: Reduce the heat to low and simmer for about 10-15 minutes, or until the raspberries have broken down, and the sauce thickens.
3. Add Mustard: Stir in the Dijon mustard and season with salt and pepper to taste. Continue to simmer for another 2-3 minutes.
4. Strain (Optional): If you prefer a smoother glaze without seeds, strain the sauce through a fine-mesh sieve to remove the seeds.
5. Cool and Store: Allow the raspberry balsamic glaze to cool to room temperature. It will thicken further as it cools. Once cooled, transfer it to an airtight container and refrigerate. It can

be stored in the refrigerator for up to two weeks.

Usage: This raspberry balsamic glaze is a versatile addition to grilled meats, salads, and roasted vegetables. It's particularly delicious drizzled over grilled chicken, pork, or a caprese salad.

Recipe 2: Raspberry BBQ Sauce for Grilled Meats
Ingredients:

- 1 cup fresh raspberries
- 1/2 cup ketchup
- 1/4 cup brown sugar
- 2 tablespoons apple cider vinegar
- 1 teaspoon smoked paprika
- 1/2 teaspoon garlic powder
- 1/2 teaspoon onion powder
- Salt and pepper to taste

Instructions:

1. Combine Ingredients: In a saucepan, combine the fresh raspberries, ketchup, brown sugar, apple cider vinegar, smoked paprika, garlic powder, onion powder, salt, and pepper.
2. Simmer: Bring the mixture to a gentle simmer over medium-low heat. Cook for about 10-15 minutes, or until the raspberries break down and the sauce thickens.
3. Blend (Optional): For a smoother sauce, you can use an immersion blender or regular blender to puree the sauce until it's smooth.
4. Cool and Store: Allow the raspberry BBQ sauce to cool to room temperature. Transfer it to an airtight container and refrigerate. It can be stored in the refrigerator for up to two weeks.

Usage: Use this raspberry BBQ sauce to enhance the flavor of grilled meats such as chicken, ribs, or pork chops. It's also a fantastic dipping sauce for chicken tenders or as a marinade for tofu and vegetables.

Recipe 3: Raspberry Chipotle Sauce for Tacos
Ingredients:

- 1 cup fresh raspberries
- 2-3 canned chipotle peppers in adobo sauce (adjust to taste)
- 1/4 cup red onion, finely chopped
- 2 tablespoons lime juice (freshly squeezed)
- 1 tablespoon honey
- Salt and pepper to taste

Instructions:

1. Combine Ingredients: In a blender or food processor, combine the fresh raspberries, chipotle peppers in adobo sauce, red onion, lime juice, honey, salt, and pepper.
2. Blend: Blend until all the ingredients are well combined and the sauce is smooth.
3. Adjust Heat: Taste the sauce and adjust the heat level by adding more chipotle peppers or adobo sauce if desired.
4. Chill: Refrigerate the raspberry chipotle sauce for at least 30 minutes before using. This allows the flavors to meld.

Usage: This raspberry chipotle sauce adds a spicy and sweet kick to tacos, grilled meats, or roasted vegetables. It's perfect for drizzling over fish tacos or using as a marinade for grilled shrimp.

These savory raspberry sauce creations are sure to impress your taste buds and dinner guests. Continue exploring the versatility of raspberry sauces in the upcoming chapters, where we'll discover even more creative uses for this delightful ingredient. Enjoy these savory delights!

Chapter 6: Raspberry Sauces in Salads

Salads can be transformed from ordinary to extraordinary with the addition of a flavorful raspberry sauce. In this chapter, we'll explore three delightful salad recipes that showcase the versatility of raspberry sauces as dressings and flavor enhancers.

Recipe 1: Raspberry Vinaigrette

Ingredients:

- 1/2 cup fresh raspberries
- 1/4 cup extra-virgin olive oil
- 2 tablespoons red wine vinegar
- 1 tablespoon honey
- 1 teaspoon Dijon mustard
- Salt and pepper to taste

Instructions:

1. Combine Ingredients: In a blender or food processor, combine the fresh raspberries, olive oil, red wine vinegar, honey, Dijon mustard, salt, and pepper.
2. Blend: Blend until all the ingredients are well combined and the vinaigrette is smooth.
3. Taste and Adjust: Taste the vinaigrette and adjust the sweetness or acidity with more honey or vinegar, as needed.
4. Chill: Refrigerate the raspberry vinaigrette for at least 30 minutes before using to allow the flavors to meld.

Usage: This raspberry vinaigrette is perfect for drizzling over mixed green salads, fruit salads, or grilled chicken salads. It adds a sweet and tangy flavor that complements a variety of ingredients.

Recipe 2: Spinach and Raspberry Salad

Ingredients:

- 6 cups fresh baby spinach
- 1 cup fresh raspberries
- 1/2 cup candied pecans or walnuts
- 1/4 cup crumbled goat cheese
- Raspberry vinaigrette (see previous recipe)

Instructions:

1. Prepare the Salad: In a large salad bowl, combine the fresh baby spinach, fresh raspberries, candied pecans or walnuts, and crumbled goat cheese.
2. Drizzle with Vinaigrette: Drizzle the raspberry vinaigrette over the salad just before serving.
3. Toss Gently: Gently toss the salad to coat the ingredients with the vinaigrette.
4. Serve: Serve the spinach and raspberry salad as a side dish or as a refreshing appetizer.

Note: You can customize this salad by adding grilled chicken or salmon for a heartier meal.

Recipe 3: Grilled Chicken Salad with Raspberry Dressing
Ingredients:
For the Raspberry Dressing:

- 1/2 cup fresh raspberries
- 1/4 cup balsamic vinegar
- 2 tablespoons extra-virgin olive oil
- 1 tablespoon honey
- 1 teaspoon Dijon mustard
- Salt and pepper to taste

For the Grilled Chicken Salad:

- 4 boneless, skinless chicken breasts
- Salt and pepper to taste
- 8 cups mixed salad greens
- 1 cup cherry tomatoes, halved
- 1/2 cup sliced cucumber
- 1/4 cup sliced red onion
- Raspberry dressing (see above)

Instructions:
For the Raspberry Dressing:

1. Combine Ingredients: In a blender or food processor, combine the fresh raspberries, balsamic vinegar, olive oil, honey, Dijon mustard, salt, and pepper.
2. Blend: Blend until all the ingredients are well combined and the dressing is smooth.
3. Taste and Adjust: Taste the dressing and adjust the sweetness or acidity with more honey or vinegar, as needed.
4. Chill: Refrigerate the raspberry dressing for at least 30 minutes before using to allow the flavors to meld.

For the Grilled Chicken Salad:

1. Preheat Grill: Preheat your grill to medium-high heat.
2. Season Chicken: Season the chicken breasts with salt and pepper.
3. Grill Chicken: Grill the chicken breasts for about 6-8 minutes per side or until they are cooked through and have grill marks. The internal temperature should reach 165°F (74°C).
4. Rest and Slice: Remove the chicken from the grill and let it rest for a few minutes before slicing it into strips.
5. Assemble Salad: In a large salad bowl, combine the mixed salad

greens, cherry tomatoes, sliced cucumber, and sliced red onion.

6. Add Chicken: Add the grilled chicken strips to the salad.
7. Drizzle with Raspberry Dressing: Drizzle the raspberry dressing over the salad and toss gently to coat.
8. Serve: Serve the grilled chicken salad with raspberry dressing as a satisfying and flavorful meal.

These raspberry sauce-infused salads are both refreshing and delicious. Whether you're looking for a light side salad or a hearty main course, these recipes offer a delightful balance of flavors. Continue exploring the world of raspberry sauces in the following chapters for more culinary inspiration. Enjoy your salads!

Chapter 7: Raspberry Sauce Cocktails

Raspberry sauce brings a burst of vibrant flavor and a touch of elegance to cocktails, making them perfect for special occasions or simply enjoying a refreshing drink. In this chapter, we'll explore three enticing raspberry sauce cocktail recipes that will elevate your mixology skills.

Recipe 1: Raspberry Mojito

Ingredients:

- 10 fresh mint leaves
- 1/2 lime, cut into wedges
- 2 teaspoons granulated sugar (adjust to taste)
- 2 tablespoons raspberry sauce
- 1/2 cup white rum
- Ice cubes
- Soda water
- Fresh raspberries and mint sprigs for garnish

Instructions:

1. Muddle Mint and Lime: In a glass, add the fresh mint leaves and lime wedges. Use a muddler or the back of a spoon to gently crush the mint leaves and release their aroma.
2. Add Sugar and Raspberry Sauce: Add the granulated sugar and raspberry sauce to the glass. Stir to combine.
3. Add Rum: Pour in the white rum and stir again.
4. Fill with Ice: Fill the glass with ice cubes.
5. Top with Soda Water: Top off the glass with soda water, filling it to your desired level.
6. Stir Gently: Give the cocktail a gentle stir to mix all the ingredients.
7. Garnish: Garnish with fresh raspberries and a sprig of mint.

8. Serve: Serve your raspberry mojito with a straw and enjoy this refreshing and fruity cocktail.

Recipe 2: Raspberry Bellini
Ingredients:

- 1/2 cup fresh raspberries
- 2 tablespoons raspberry sauce
- 1 bottle (750ml) chilled sparkling wine or prosecco
- Fresh raspberries for garnish

Instructions:

1. Blend Raspberries: In a blender or food processor, puree the fresh raspberries until smooth.
2. Strain (Optional): If desired, strain the raspberry puree through a fine-mesh sieve to remove the seeds.
3. Mix with Raspberry Sauce: In a pitcher, combine the raspberry puree and raspberry sauce.
4. Pour Sparkling Wine: Pour the chilled sparkling wine or prosecco into the pitcher with the raspberry mixture. Stir gently to combine.
5. Serve: Pour the raspberry bellini into chilled glasses and garnish with fresh raspberries.
6. Enjoy: Raise your glass and enjoy this elegant and fruity cocktail.

Recipe 3: Raspberry Whiskey Sour
Ingredients:

- 2 ounces bourbon or whiskey
- 1 ounce freshly squeezed lemon juice
- 1/2 ounce simple syrup
- 1 tablespoon raspberry sauce

- Ice cubes
- Fresh raspberries and lemon slice for garnish

Instructions:

1. Prepare the Cocktail: In a cocktail shaker, combine the bourbon or whiskey, freshly squeezed lemon juice, simple syrup, and raspberry sauce.
2. Add Ice: Add ice cubes to the shaker.
3. Shake: Shake the cocktail vigorously until well-chilled.
4. Strain and Serve: Strain the cocktail into a rocks glass filled with ice.
5. Garnish: Garnish with fresh raspberries and a slice of lemon.
6. Enjoy: Sip and savor the sweet and tangy flavors of your raspberry whiskey sour.

These raspberry sauce cocktails offer a delightful blend of fruity and alcoholic flavors, making them perfect for cocktail enthusiasts and anyone looking to add a touch of sophistication to their gatherings. Continue exploring the world of raspberry sauces in the following chapters for even more culinary inspiration. Enjoy responsibly!

Chapter 8: Raspberry Sauce in Beverages

Raspberry sauce adds a burst of fruity flavor to a variety of beverages, from refreshing lemonades to thirst-quenching iced teas and creamy smoothies. In this chapter, we'll explore three delightful raspberry sauce beverage recipes to quench your thirst.

Recipe 1: Raspberry Lemonade

Ingredients:

- 1 cup fresh raspberries
- 1/2 cup granulated sugar (adjust to taste)
- 1 cup freshly squeezed lemon juice
- 4 cups cold water
- Ice cubes
- Fresh lemon slices and raspberries for garnish
- Mint sprigs (optional)

Instructions:

1. Prepare Raspberry Puree: In a blender or food processor, puree the fresh raspberries until smooth.
2. Strain (Optional): If desired, strain the raspberry puree through a fine-mesh sieve to remove the seeds.
3. Combine Ingredients: In a pitcher, combine the raspberry puree, granulated sugar, freshly squeezed lemon juice, and cold water. Stir until the sugar is dissolved.
4. Chill: Refrigerate the raspberry lemonade for at least 30 minutes to allow the flavors to meld.
5. Serve: Fill glasses with ice cubes and pour the raspberry lemonade over the ice. Garnish with fresh lemon slices, raspberries, and mint sprigs if desired.
6. Enjoy: Sip and enjoy the refreshing and tangy flavors of

raspberry lemonade on a hot day.

Recipe 2: Raspberry Iced Tea
Ingredients:

- 4 cups brewed black tea, cooled
- 1/2 cup raspberry sauce
- 1/4 cup honey (adjust to taste)
- Ice cubes
- Fresh raspberries and lemon slices for garnish
- Mint sprigs (optional)

Instructions:

1. Prepare Brewed Tea: Brew 4 cups of black tea and let it cool to room temperature.
2. Combine Ingredients: In a pitcher, combine the brewed black tea, raspberry sauce, and honey. Stir until the honey is dissolved.
3. Chill: Refrigerate the raspberry iced tea for at least 30 minutes to allow the flavors to meld.
4. Serve: Fill glasses with ice cubes and pour the raspberry iced tea over the ice. Garnish with fresh raspberries, lemon slices, and mint sprigs if desired.
5. Enjoy: Sip and relish the sweet and fruity flavors of raspberry iced tea.

Recipe 3: Raspberry Smoothies
Ingredients:

- 1 cup fresh raspberries
- 1/2 cup raspberry sauce
- 1 cup Greek yogurt
- 1 banana
- 1/2 cup milk (adjust to desired thickness)

- 1 tablespoon honey (adjust to taste)
- Ice cubes

Instructions:

1. Blend Ingredients: In a blender, combine the fresh raspberries, raspberry sauce, Greek yogurt, banana, milk, and honey.
2. Add Ice: Add ice cubes to the blender to achieve the desired thickness and consistency.
3. Blend: Blend until all the ingredients are well combined and the smoothie is creamy and smooth.
4. Taste and Adjust: Taste the smoothie and adjust the sweetness with more honey, if needed.
5. Serve: Pour the raspberry smoothie into glasses and enjoy it as a refreshing and nutritious drink.

These raspberry sauce beverages offer a delightful way to enjoy the sweet and tart flavors of raspberries in a variety of refreshing and satisfying drinks. Continue exploring the world of raspberry sauces in the following chapters for even more culinary inspiration. Cheers!

Chapter 9: Raspberry Sauces for Brunch

Brunch is a delightful occasion to enjoy both savory and sweet dishes, and raspberry sauces can add a burst of fruity flavor to your brunch creations. In this chapter, we'll explore three mouthwatering brunch recipes that incorporate raspberry sauces.

Recipe 1: Raspberry Stuffed French Toast

Ingredients:

For the French Toast:

- 8 slices of thick bread (such as challah or brioche)
- 4 ounces cream cheese, softened
- 1/2 cup fresh raspberries
- 2 large eggs
- 1/2 cup milk
- 1 teaspoon vanilla extract
- 2 tablespoons granulated sugar
- Butter for cooking

For the Raspberry Sauce:

- 1 cup fresh raspberries
- 1/4 cup raspberry sauce
- 2 tablespoons maple syrup

Instructions:

For the French Toast:

Prepare Cream Cheese Filling: In a bowl, combine the softened cream cheese and fresh raspberries. Mash the raspberries into the cream cheese until well combined.

Make Sandwiches: Spread the cream cheese and raspberry mixture evenly onto 4 slices of bread. Top each with another slice of bread to make sandwiches.

Whisk Egg Mixture: In a separate bowl, whisk together the eggs, milk, vanilla extract, and granulated sugar.

Dip and Cook: Heat a skillet or griddle over medium heat and melt some butter. Dip each sandwich into the egg mixture, ensuring both sides are coated, and cook until golden brown on each side.

For the Raspberry Sauce:

Combine Ingredients: In a saucepan, combine the fresh raspberries, raspberry sauce, and maple syrup. Heat over low heat until the raspberries break down and the sauce is warmed through.

Serve: Serve the raspberry stuffed French toast with warm raspberry sauce drizzled over the top.

Recipe 2: Raspberry Danish Pastry
Ingredients:

- 1 sheet puff pastry (thawed if frozen)
- 4 ounces cream cheese, softened
- 1/4 cup granulated sugar
- 1/2 teaspoon vanilla extract
- 1/2 cup fresh raspberries
- Raspberry sauce (for drizzling)

Instructions:

1. Preheat Oven: Preheat your oven to 375°F (190°C) and line a baking sheet with parchment paper.
2. Prepare Puff Pastry: Roll out the puff pastry sheet onto the prepared baking sheet.
3. Make Cream Cheese Filling: In a bowl, combine the softened cream cheese, granulated sugar, and vanilla extract. Spread this mixture evenly over the center of the puff pastry, leaving a border around the edges.

4. Add Raspberries: Sprinkle the fresh raspberries over the cream cheese filling.
5. Fold and Bake: Carefully fold the edges of the puff pastry over the filling, creating a border. Bake in the preheated oven for 20-25 minutes or until the pastry is golden brown and puffed up.
6. Serve: Once the Danish pastry has cooled slightly, drizzle it with raspberry sauce. Slice and serve.

Recipe 3: Raspberry Mimosas
Ingredients:

- 1 bottle of chilled champagne or sparkling wine
- 1/2 cup raspberry sauce
- Fresh raspberries for garnish
- Fresh mint leaves for garnish

Instructions:

1. Prepare Champagne Flutes: Chill champagne flutes in the refrigerator for at least 30 minutes before serving.
2. Add Raspberry Sauce: In each chilled flute, add 1-2 tablespoons of raspberry sauce.
3. Pour Champagne: Pour the chilled champagne or sparkling wine into the flutes, filling them about two-thirds full.
4. Garnish: Garnish with fresh raspberries and a mint leaf in each glass.
5. Serve: Serve raspberry mimosas as a delightful and sparkling brunch cocktail.

These raspberry sauce brunch recipes are perfect for a leisurely weekend brunch or any special occasion. Whether you prefer sweet or savory, these dishes offer a burst of fruity flavor to enhance your brunch experience. Enjoy!

Chapter 10: Raspberry Sauces for Special Occasions

Raspberry sauces add a touch of elegance and sophistication to special occasions and celebrations. In this chapter, we'll explore three exquisite raspberry sauce recipes that are perfect for making your special moments even more memorable.

Recipe 1: Raspberry Champagne Sauce for Celebration
Ingredients:

- 1 cup fresh raspberries
- 1/4 cup granulated sugar (adjust to taste)
- 1/4 cup champagne or sparkling wine
- 1/4 cup raspberry sauce

Instructions:

1. Combine Ingredients: In a saucepan, combine the fresh raspberries, granulated sugar, champagne or sparkling wine, and raspberry sauce.
2. Simmer: Bring the mixture to a gentle simmer over medium heat. Stir occasionally and let it simmer for about 10-15 minutes, or until the raspberries break down and the sauce thickens.
3. Strain (Optional): If you prefer a smoother sauce without seeds, strain the sauce through a fine-mesh sieve to remove the raspberry seeds.
4. Cool: Allow the raspberry champagne sauce to cool to room temperature.
5. Serve: Drizzle the sauce over desserts like cheesecakes, ice cream, or chocolate mousse for a touch of luxury during your celebration.

Recipe 2: Raspberry Sauce for Wedding Cakes
Ingredients:

- 2 cups fresh raspberries
- 1/2 cup raspberry sauce
- 1/4 cup granulated sugar (adjust to taste)
- 1 tablespoon lemon juice

Instructions:

1. Combine Ingredients: In a saucepan, combine the fresh raspberries, raspberry sauce, granulated sugar, and lemon juice.
2. Simmer: Bring the mixture to a gentle simmer over medium heat. Stir occasionally and let it simmer for about 10-15 minutes, or until the raspberries break down and the sauce thickens.
3. Strain (Optional): For a smooth sauce without seeds, strain the sauce through a fine-mesh sieve to remove the raspberry seeds.
4. Cool: Allow the raspberry sauce to cool to room temperature.
5. Use for Wedding Cakes: Drizzle or spread the raspberry sauce between the layers of a wedding cake or as a decorative garnish. Its vibrant color and sweet-tart flavor will make your wedding cake truly special.

Recipe 3: Raspberry Chocolate Fondue
Ingredients:

- 1 cup semisweet chocolate chips
- 1/2 cup heavy cream
- 1/4 cup raspberry sauce
- Assorted dippers (strawberries, marshmallows, pretzels, etc.)

Instructions:

1. Prepare Fondue Pot: Set up a fondue pot or a double boiler.
2. Combine Ingredients: In a heatproof bowl, combine the semisweet chocolate chips, heavy cream, and raspberry sauce.
3. Melt Chocolate: Place the bowl over simmering water in the fondue pot or double boiler. Stir until the chocolate chips are fully melted and the mixture is smooth and glossy.
4. Serve: Transfer the raspberry chocolate fondue to a fondue pot with a tea light or low heat source to keep it warm. Serve with a variety of dippers for a fun and interactive dessert experience.

These raspberry sauce recipes are perfect for adding a touch of elegance and flavor to your special occasions, from celebrations to weddings and romantic evenings. The sweet and tangy raspberry sauce complements a variety of desserts and treats, making them even more memorable. Enjoy these recipes on your special days!

Chapter 11: Raspberry Sauces for the Grill

Raspberry sauces can add a burst of flavor and a touch of sweetness to grilled dishes, enhancing their smoky and savory profiles. In this chapter, we'll explore three delectable raspberry sauce recipes that are perfect for grilling.

Recipe 1: Raspberry BBQ Ribs
Ingredients:
For the Ribs:

- 2 racks of baby back ribs
- Salt and pepper to taste
- 1 cup raspberry sauce

For the BBQ Sauce:

- 1 cup raspberry sauce
- 1/2 cup ketchup
- 1/4 cup apple cider vinegar
- 1/4 cup brown sugar
- 2 tablespoons Worcestershire sauce
- 1 tablespoon Dijon mustard
- 1 teaspoon smoked paprika
- 1/2 teaspoon garlic powder
- 1/2 teaspoon onion powder
- Salt and pepper to taste

Instructions:
For the Ribs:

1. Preheat Grill: Preheat your grill to medium-high heat.
2. Season Ribs: Season the racks of baby back ribs generously with

salt and pepper.

3. Grill Ribs: Place the ribs on the grill and cook for about 25-30 minutes per side, basting with raspberry sauce during the last 5 minutes of grilling.

For the BBQ Sauce:

1. Combine Ingredients: In a saucepan, combine the raspberry sauce, ketchup, apple cider vinegar, brown sugar, Worcestershire sauce, Dijon mustard, smoked paprika, garlic powder, onion powder, salt, and pepper.
2. Simmer and Reduce: Bring the sauce to a simmer over medium heat and let it cook for about 15-20 minutes, or until it thickens and the flavors meld. Stir occasionally.
3. Glaze Ribs: During the last 5 minutes of grilling, brush the ribs with the raspberry BBQ sauce on both sides. Continue grilling until the sauce caramelizes and forms a delicious glaze.
4. Serve: Slice the ribs and serve with extra raspberry BBQ sauce on the side.

Recipe 2: Raspberry Glazed Salmon
Ingredients:

- 4 salmon fillets
- Salt and pepper to taste
- Olive oil for grilling
- 1/2 cup raspberry sauce
- 1 tablespoon lemon juice
- 1 tablespoon honey
- 1 teaspoon Dijon mustard

Instructions:

1. Preheat Grill: Preheat your grill to medium-high heat and brush the grates with oil to prevent sticking.
2. Season Salmon: Season the salmon fillets with salt and pepper.
3. Grill Salmon: Place the salmon fillets on the grill, skin-side down. Grill for about 4-5 minutes per side, or until the salmon is cooked to your desired level of doneness and has grill marks.
4. Prepare Raspberry Glaze: In a saucepan, combine the raspberry sauce, lemon juice, honey, and Dijon mustard. Heat over low heat, stirring until well combined and heated through.
5. Glaze Salmon: Brush the raspberry glaze over the grilled salmon fillets during the last minute of grilling. Let it caramelize slightly.
6. Serve: Remove the salmon from the grill, drizzle with any remaining glaze, and serve immediately.

Recipe 3: Grilled Portobello Mushrooms with Raspberry Drizzle
Ingredients:

- 4 large Portobello mushrooms, cleaned and stems removed

- Olive oil for brushing
- Salt and pepper to taste
- 1/2 cup raspberry sauce
- 2 tablespoons balsamic vinegar
- Fresh basil leaves for garnish

Instructions:

1. Preheat Grill: Preheat your grill to medium-high heat.
2. Brush Mushrooms: Brush both sides of the Portobello mushrooms with olive oil and season with salt and pepper.
3. Grill Mushrooms: Place the mushrooms on the grill, gill-side down. Grill for about 4-5 minutes per side, or until they are tender and have grill marks.
4. Prepare Raspberry Drizzle: In a small bowl, whisk together the raspberry sauce and balsamic vinegar.
5. Serve: Remove the grilled Portobello mushrooms from the grill, drizzle with the raspberry sauce mixture, and garnish with fresh basil leaves.

These raspberry sauce grill recipes are perfect for adding a burst of fruity flavor to your grilled dishes, whether you're cooking up ribs, seafood, or vegetables. The sweet and tangy raspberry sauces complement the smoky flavors of the grill, creating a delightful culinary experience. Enjoy your grilled creations!

Chapter 12: Raspberry Sauces for Healthy Eating

Raspberry sauces can enhance the flavor and nutritional value of healthy dishes, making them even more enticing. In this chapter, we'll explore three nutritious and delicious raspberry sauce recipes that are perfect for maintaining a balanced and healthy diet.

Recipe 1: Raspberry Chia Seed Pudding

Ingredients:

- 1/4 cup chia seeds
- 1 cup almond milk (or your choice of milk)
- 2 tablespoons raspberry sauce
- 1/2 teaspoon vanilla extract
- Fresh raspberries for garnish
- Sliced almonds for garnish

Instructions:

1. Combine Ingredients: In a bowl, combine the chia seeds, almond milk, raspberry sauce, and vanilla extract. Stir well.
2. Chill: Cover the bowl and refrigerate for at least 2 hours or overnight, allowing the chia seeds to absorb the liquid and thicken.
3. Stir: Stir the chia seed pudding to ensure an even consistency.
4. Serve: Divide the pudding into serving cups or bowls. Top with fresh raspberries and sliced almonds.

Enjoy: Enjoy a healthy and filling raspberry chia seed pudding as a nutritious breakfast or snack.

Recipe 2: Quinoa Salad with Raspberry Dressing

Ingredients:

For the Salad:

- 1 cup quinoa, cooked and cooled
- 1 cup fresh raspberries
- 1 cup cucumber, diced
- 1 cup cherry tomatoes, halved
- 1/4 cup red onion, finely chopped
- 1/4 cup fresh basil leaves, chopped
- 1/4 cup feta cheese (optional)
- Salt and pepper to taste

For the Raspberry Dressing:

- 1/2 cup fresh raspberries
- 2 tablespoons raspberry sauce
- 2 tablespoons olive oil
- 1 tablespoon balsamic vinegar
- 1 tablespoon honey
- Salt and pepper to taste

Instructions:

For the Salad:

Combine Ingredients: In a large salad bowl, combine the cooked and cooled quinoa, fresh raspberries, diced cucumber, cherry tomatoes, red onion, chopped basil, and feta cheese (if using).

Season: Season the salad with salt and pepper to taste.

For the Raspberry Dressing:

Blend Ingredients: In a blender or food processor, combine the fresh raspberries, raspberry sauce, olive oil, balsamic vinegar, honey, salt, and pepper. Blend until the dressing is smooth.

Dress Salad: Drizzle the raspberry dressing over the quinoa salad and toss gently to combine.

Serve: Serve the quinoa salad with raspberry dressing as a nutritious and flavorful meal.

Recipe 3: Raspberry Green Smoothie Bowl
Ingredients:

- 1 cup fresh spinach or kale leaves
- 1/2 cup fresh raspberries
- 1/2 cup frozen banana slices
- 1/2 cup unsweetened almond milk (or your choice of milk)
- 2 tablespoons raspberry sauce
- Toppings: Fresh raspberries, sliced kiwi, granola, chia seeds, and shredded coconut

Instructions:

1. Blend Ingredients: In a blender, combine the fresh spinach or kale leaves, fresh raspberries, frozen banana slices, almond milk, and raspberry sauce. Blend until smooth and creamy.
2. Prepare Bowl: Pour the green smoothie into a bowl.
3. Add Toppings: Top the smoothie bowl with fresh raspberries, sliced kiwi, granola, chia seeds, and shredded coconut. Customize it with your favorite toppings.
4. Enjoy: Enjoy your raspberry green smoothie bowl as a nutrient-packed and refreshing breakfast or snack.

These raspberry sauce recipes for healthy eating offer a delightful way to incorporate the sweet and tart flavors of raspberries into your diet while enjoying nutritious and satisfying dishes. Whether it's a chia seed pudding, a quinoa salad, or a green smoothie bowl, these recipes make healthy eating a delicious experience. Enjoy!

Chapter 13: Raspberry Sauces for International Flavors

Raspberry sauces can add an exotic twist to dishes inspired by cuisines from around the world. In this chapter, we'll explore three unique raspberry sauce recipes that capture the essence of Mexican, Thai, and Indian flavors.

Recipe 1: Raspberry Salsa for Mexican Cuisine

Ingredients:

- 1 cup fresh raspberries
- 1/2 cup diced red onion
- 1/2 cup diced tomatoes
- 1/4 cup chopped fresh cilantro
- 1 jalapeño pepper, finely chopped (adjust to taste)
- 1 clove garlic, minced
- Juice of 1 lime
- Salt and pepper to taste
- Tortilla chips for serving

Instructions:

1. Prepare Raspberry Salsa: In a bowl, gently combine the fresh raspberries, diced red onion, diced tomatoes, chopped cilantro, chopped jalapeño pepper, minced garlic, and lime juice.
2. Season: Season the salsa with salt and pepper to taste. Adjust the level of spiciness by adding more or less jalapeño pepper.
3. Chill: Cover the bowl and refrigerate the raspberry salsa for at least 30 minutes before serving to allow the flavors to meld.
4. Serve: Serve the raspberry salsa as a unique and fruity twist on traditional Mexican salsa. It pairs perfectly with tortilla chips or as a topping for tacos and grilled meats.

Recipe 2: Thai-Inspired Raspberry Dipping Sauce
Ingredients:

- 1 cup fresh raspberries
- 1/4 cup sweet chili sauce
- 2 tablespoons fish sauce
- 2 tablespoons lime juice
- 1 tablespoon brown sugar (adjust to taste)
- 1 clove garlic, minced
- 1 teaspoon grated fresh ginger
- Crushed red pepper flakes (optional, for extra heat)

Instructions:

1. Prepare Raspberry Dipping Sauce: In a blender or food processor, combine the fresh raspberries, sweet chili sauce, fish sauce, lime juice, brown sugar, minced garlic, and grated ginger.
2. Blend: Blend until all the ingredients are well combined and the sauce is smooth. For extra heat, add crushed red pepper flakes to taste.
3. Taste and Adjust: Taste the dipping sauce and adjust the sweetness or spiciness by adding more brown sugar or red pepper flakes, if desired.
4. Serve: Serve the Thai-inspired raspberry dipping sauce with your favorite Thai appetizers like spring rolls, satay, or as a dipping sauce for grilled shrimp and chicken.

Recipe 3: Indian Raspberry Chutney
Ingredients:

- 1 cup fresh raspberries
- 1/2 cup diced red onion
- 1/4 cup raisins
- 1/4 cup apple cider vinegar

- 2 tablespoons brown sugar (adjust to taste)
- 1 teaspoon grated fresh ginger
- 1/2 teaspoon ground cinnamon
- 1/4 teaspoon ground cloves
- Salt to taste

Instructions:

1. Prepare Raspberry Chutney: In a saucepan, combine the fresh raspberries, diced red onion, raisins, apple cider vinegar, brown sugar, grated ginger, ground cinnamon, and ground cloves.
2. Simmer: Bring the mixture to a simmer over medium heat. Reduce the heat to low and let it cook for about 20-25 minutes, stirring occasionally, until the chutney thickens and the raspberries break down.
3. Season: Season the raspberry chutney with salt to taste and adjust the sweetness with more brown sugar if needed.
4. Cool: Allow the chutney to cool to room temperature.
5. Serve: Serve the Indian-inspired raspberry chutney as a condiment with Indian dishes, grilled meats, or as a delightful addition to cheese platters.

These raspberry sauce recipes with international flavors offer a culinary journey to different parts of the world. From the zesty Mexican salsa to the sweet and spicy Thai dipping sauce and the aromatic Indian chutney, these recipes allow you to explore a diverse range of global tastes using raspberries as a unique ingredient. Enjoy the fusion of flavors!

Chapter 14: Raspberry Sauces for Snacking

Raspberry sauces can transform your everyday snacks into delightful and flavorful treats. In this chapter, we'll explore three raspberry sauce recipes that are perfect for snacking, whether you're looking for energy-boosting bites, a creamy dip, or satisfying granola bars.

Recipe 1: Raspberry Almond Energy Bites
Ingredients:

- 1 cup rolled oats
- 1/2 cup almond butter
- 1/4 cup honey
- 1/4 cup raspberry sauce
- 1/4 cup sliced almonds
- 1/4 cup dried cranberries
- 1/4 teaspoon vanilla extract
- Pinch of salt
- Shredded coconut for rolling (optional)

Instructions:

1. Combine Ingredients: In a mixing bowl, combine the rolled oats, almond butter, honey, raspberry sauce, sliced almonds, dried cranberries, vanilla extract, and a pinch of salt. Mix until all the ingredients are well combined.
2. Chill Mixture: Cover the mixture and refrigerate for about 30 minutes to make it easier to handle.
3. Roll into Bites: After chilling, use your hands to roll the mixture into small energy bites, about 1 inch in diameter.
4. Optional Coating: If desired, roll the energy bites in shredded coconut for added texture and flavor.

5. Chill Again: Place the energy bites on a baking sheet lined with parchment paper and refrigerate for an additional 15-20 minutes to firm up.

6. Store and Enjoy: Store the raspberry almond energy bites in an airtight container in the refrigerator. Enjoy them as a quick and nutritious snack.

Recipe 2: Raspberry Yogurt Dip
Ingredients:

- 1/2 cup Greek yogurt
- 1/4 cup raspberry sauce
- 1 tablespoon honey (adjust to taste)
- Fresh fruit for dipping (strawberries, apple slices, banana, etc.)

Instructions:

1. Prepare Raspberry Yogurt Dip: In a bowl, combine the Greek yogurt, raspberry sauce, and honey. Mix until well combined.

2. Taste and Adjust: Taste the yogurt dip and adjust the sweetness with more honey if desired.

3. Chill: Refrigerate the raspberry yogurt dip for at least 30 minutes to allow the flavors to meld.

4. Serve: Serve the dip with fresh fruit for a delicious and healthy snacking option.

Recipe 3: Raspberry Granola Bars
Ingredients:

- 2 cups rolled oats
- 1/2 cup almond butter
- 1/4 cup honey
- 1/4 cup raspberry sauce
- 1/4 cup sliced almonds

- 1/4 cup dried raspberries (or other dried fruit of your choice)
- 1/4 teaspoon vanilla extract
- Pinch of salt

Instructions:

1. Preheat Oven: Preheat your oven to 350°F (175°C). Grease an 8x8-inch baking pan and line it with parchment paper, leaving an overhang on two sides.
2. Mix Ingredients: In a large mixing bowl, combine the rolled oats, almond butter, honey, raspberry sauce, sliced almonds, dried raspberries, vanilla extract, and a pinch of salt. Mix until all the ingredients are well combined.
3. Press into Pan: Transfer the mixture to the prepared baking pan and press it down firmly into an even layer.
4. Bake: Bake in the preheated oven for 20-25 minutes, or until the granola bars are lightly golden on the edges.
5. Cool and Cut: Allow the bars to cool completely in the pan. Once cooled, use the parchment paper overhangs to lift the bars out of the pan. Place them on a cutting board and cut into individual bars.
6. Store and Enjoy: Store the raspberry granola bars in an airtight container for snacking on the go or as a quick energy boost during your day.

These raspberry sauce snack recipes offer a delightful way to enjoy the sweet and tangy flavors of raspberries while satisfying your cravings for delicious and nutritious snacks. Whether it's energy bites, a creamy yogurt dip, or granola bars, these recipes are perfect for your snacking pleasure. Enjoy!

Chapter 15: Raspberry Sauces for Kids

Raspberry sauces can make mealtime more fun and appealing for kids. In this chapter, we'll explore three kid-friendly raspberry sauce recipes that are sure to please young palates.

Recipe 1: Peanut Butter and Raspberry Sandwiches
Ingredients:

- 4 slices of whole-grain bread
- 2 tablespoons peanut butter (or almond butter for nut-free option)
- 2 tablespoons raspberry sauce
- Banana slices (optional)

Instructions:

1. Prepare Bread: Lay out the slices of whole-grain bread on a clean surface.
2. Spread Peanut Butter: Spread peanut butter evenly on two of the bread slices.
3. Add Raspberry Sauce: Spread raspberry sauce on the other two bread slices.
4. Optional Banana: If desired, add banana slices to the peanut butter side.
5. Create Sandwiches: Pair up the peanut butter and raspberry sauce slices to create two sandwiches.
6. Cut and Serve: Cut the sandwiches into halves or quarters for kid-sized portions. Serve as a tasty and wholesome snack or lunch option.

Recipe 2: Raspberry Applesauce

Ingredients:

- 4 cups unsweetened applesauce
- 1/2 cup raspberry sauce
- Cinnamon (optional, for added flavor)

Instructions:

1. Combine Ingredients: In a mixing bowl, combine the unsweetened applesauce and raspberry sauce. Mix until well combined.
2. Optional Cinnamon: If desired, sprinkle a pinch of cinnamon into the mixture for extra flavor.
3. Stir Well: Stir the raspberry applesauce until the raspberry sauce is evenly distributed throughout the applesauce.
4. Chill: Refrigerate the raspberry applesauce for a refreshing and fruity treat.
5. Serve: Serve the raspberry applesauce as a healthy and delicious snack or dessert option for kids.

Recipe 3: Raspberry Yogurt Popsicles
Ingredients:

- 1 cup Greek yogurt
- 1/2 cup raspberry sauce
- 2 tablespoons honey (adjust to taste)
- Fresh raspberries (optional, for added texture)

Instructions:

1. Prepare Yogurt Mixture: In a mixing bowl, combine the Greek yogurt, raspberry sauce, and honey. Mix until smooth and well combined.
2. Optional Raspberries: If desired, gently fold in some fresh raspberries for added texture.
3. Fill Popsicle Molds: Pour the raspberry yogurt mixture into popsicle molds, leaving a little space at the top for expansion.
4. Insert Sticks: Insert popsicle sticks into each mold.
5. Freeze: Place the popsicle molds in the freezer and freeze for at least 4 hours or until the popsicles are completely frozen.
6. Unmold and Serve: To unmold the popsicles, run the molds briefly under warm water to loosen them. Serve the raspberry yogurt popsicles as a delightful and healthy frozen treat for kids.

These raspberry sauce recipes for kids are designed to be both tasty and appealing to young taste buds. Whether it's a peanut butter and raspberry sandwich, raspberry applesauce, or yogurt popsicles, these recipes offer a playful way to introduce the sweet and tangy flavors of raspberries to children while providing them with nutritious options for snacks and meals. Enjoy!

Chapter 16: Raspberry Sauces for Baking

Raspberry sauces can infuse your baked goods with a burst of fruity flavor and add a touch of sweetness. In this chapter, we'll explore three delightful raspberry sauce recipes that are perfect for baking delicious treats.

Recipe 1: Raspberry-Filled Donuts
Ingredients:
For the Donuts:

- 2 cups all-purpose flour
- 1/2 cup granulated sugar
- 1 teaspoon baking powder
- 1/2 teaspoon baking soda
- 1/2 teaspoon salt
- 1/2 cup buttermilk
- 1/2 cup Greek yogurt
- 2 large eggs
- 2 tablespoons unsalted butter, melted
- 1 teaspoon vanilla extract
- Raspberry sauce for filling (about 1/2 cup)
- Vegetable oil for frying

For the Glaze:

- 1 cup powdered sugar
- 2-3 tablespoons milk
- 1/2 teaspoon vanilla extract

Instructions:
For the Donuts:

1. Prepare Donut Batter: In a large mixing bowl, whisk together

the all-purpose flour, granulated sugar, baking powder, baking soda, and salt.

2. Add Wet Ingredients: In another bowl, whisk together the buttermilk, Greek yogurt, eggs, melted butter, and vanilla extract.

3. Combine: Pour the wet ingredients into the dry ingredients and stir until just combined. Be careful not to overmix; the batter should be lumpy.

4. Fill Donut Pan: Fill a donut pan with the batter, filling each cavity about 2/3 full.

5. Bake: Bake in a preheated oven according to the donut pan's instructions until the donuts are lightly golden and a toothpick inserted into one comes out clean.

6. Cool: Allow the donuts to cool in the pan for a few minutes before transferring them to a wire rack to cool completely.

7. Fill Donuts: Once the donuts are cool, use a piping bag or plastic squeeze bottle to inject raspberry sauce into the center of each donut.

For the Glaze:

1. Prepare Glaze: In a bowl, whisk together the powdered sugar, milk, and vanilla extract until smooth and the desired consistency is reached.

2. Glaze Donuts: Dip each raspberry-filled donut into the glaze, allowing any excess to drip off. Place them on a wire rack to let the glaze set.

1. Serve: Enjoy your raspberry-filled donuts as a sweet and fruity treat.

Recipe 2: Raspberry Swirl Bread
Ingredients:

- 2 cups all-purpose flour
- 1 teaspoon baking powder
- 1/2 teaspoon baking soda
- 1/2 teaspoon salt
- 1/2 cup unsalted butter, softened
- 1 cup granulated sugar
- 2 large eggs
- 1 teaspoon vanilla extract
- 1 cup buttermilk
- 1/2 cup raspberry sauce

Instructions:

1. Preheat Oven: Preheat your oven to 350°F (175°C). Grease and flour a 9x5-inch loaf pan.
2. Mix Dry Ingredients: In a mixing bowl, whisk together the all-purpose flour, baking powder, baking soda, and salt.
3. Cream Butter and Sugar: In another bowl, cream together the softened unsalted butter and granulated sugar until light and fluffy.
4. Add Eggs and Vanilla: Beat in the eggs one at a time, then stir in the vanilla extract.
5. Alternate Dry and Wet Ingredients: Gradually add the dry ingredients to the butter mixture, alternating with buttermilk, beginning and ending with the dry ingredients. Mix until just combined.
6. Swirl in Raspberry Sauce: Gently fold in the raspberry sauce, creating a swirling pattern but avoiding overmixing.
7. Transfer to Pan: Pour the batter into the prepared loaf pan.
8. Bake: Bake in the preheated oven for 50-60 minutes, or until a

toothpick inserted into the center comes out clean.

9. Cool and Serve: Allow the raspberry swirl bread to cool in the pan for about 10 minutes before transferring it to a wire rack to cool completely. Slice and enjoy as a delightful raspberry-infused bread.

Recipe 3: Raspberry-Filled Cupcakes
Ingredients:
For the Cupcakes:

- 1 1/2 cups all-purpose flour
- 1 1/2 teaspoons baking powder
- 1/4 teaspoon salt
- 1/2 cup unsalted butter, softened
- 1 cup granulated sugar
- 2 large eggs
- 1 teaspoon vanilla extract
- 1/2 cup milk
- Raspberry sauce for filling (about 1/2 cup)

For the Frosting:

- 1/2 cup unsalted butter, softened
- 2 cups powdered sugar
- 1/4 cup raspberry sauce
- Fresh raspberries for garnish (optional)

Instructions:
For the Cupcakes:

1. Preheat Oven: Preheat your oven to 350°F (175°C). Line a muffin tin with cupcake liners.
2. Mix Dry Ingredients: In a mixing bowl, whisk together the all-purpose flour, baking powder, and salt.
3. Cream Butter and Sugar: In another bowl, cream together the softened unsalted butter and granulated sugar until light and fluffy.
4. Add Eggs and Vanilla: Beat in the eggs one at a time, then stir in the vanilla extract.
5. Alternate Dry and Wet Ingredients: Gradually add the dry

ingredients to the butter mixture, alternating with milk, beginning and ending with the dry ingredients. Mix until just combined.

6. Fill Cupcake Liners: Fill each cupcake liner about 2/3 full with the cupcake batter.

7. Bake: Bake in the preheated oven for 18-20 minutes, or until a toothpick inserted into a cupcake comes out clean.

8. Cool: Allow the cupcakes to cool in the muffin tin for a few minutes before transferring them to a wire rack to cool completely.

9. Fill Cupcakes: Once the cupcakes are cool, use a piping bag or a cupcake corer to fill the center of each cupcake with raspberry sauce.

Chapter 17: Raspberry Sauces for Cheese Platters

Raspberry sauces can elevate your cheese platters to a whole new level by providing a sweet and tangy contrast to the richness of various cheeses. In this chapter, we'll explore three delightful raspberry sauce recipes that pair beautifully with a selection of cheeses.

Recipe 1: Raspberry and Brie Crostini
Ingredients:

- Baguette or French bread, sliced into crostini rounds
- 1 wheel of Brie cheese, cut into thin slices
- Raspberry sauce
- Fresh basil leaves for garnish

Instructions:

1. Toast Crostini: Preheat your oven to 350°F (175°C). Arrange the sliced baguette or French bread rounds on a baking sheet and toast them in the oven until they become crisp and lightly golden.
2. Assemble Crostini: Place a slice of Brie cheese on each toasted crostini round.
3. Drizzle with Raspberry Sauce: Drizzle raspberry sauce over the Brie-topped crostinis.
4. Garnish: Garnish each crostini with a fresh basil leaf.
5. Serve: Arrange the raspberry and Brie crostinis on a serving platter and serve as an elegant and flavorful addition to your cheese platter.

Recipe 2: Raspberry Goat Cheese Spread
Ingredients:

- 4 oz goat cheese
- 2 tablespoons raspberry sauce
- 1 tablespoon honey (adjust to taste)
- Crackers or crusty bread for serving
- Fresh raspberries for garnish (optional)

Instructions:

1. Prepare Goat Cheese Spread: In a bowl, combine the goat cheese, raspberry sauce, and honey. Mix until well blended and smooth. Adjust the sweetness with more honey if desired.
2. Serve: Transfer the raspberry goat cheese spread to a serving bowl.
3. Garnish: If desired, garnish the spread with fresh raspberries.
4. Serve: Serve the raspberry goat cheese spread with crackers or slices of crusty bread as a creamy and fruity addition to your cheese platter.

Recipe 3: Raspberry and Gouda Pairing
Ingredients:

- Gouda cheese, sliced into wedges or cubes
- Raspberry sauce
- Toasted almond slices for garnish (optional)

Instructions:

1. Prepare Gouda Cheese: Arrange slices of Gouda cheese on a cheese platter or board.
2. Drizzle with Raspberry Sauce: Drizzle raspberry sauce over the Gouda cheese slices or cubes.
3. Garnish: If desired, garnish the raspberry and Gouda pairing with toasted almond slices for added texture and flavor.
4. Serve: Serve the raspberry and Gouda pairing as a simple yet delightful combination that showcases the sweet and savory contrast of flavors.

These raspberry sauce recipes for cheese platters offer a wonderful way to complement and enhance the flavors of various cheeses. Whether you're indulging in creamy Brie, tangy goat cheese, or nutty Gouda, these raspberry sauce pairings create a harmonious balance of tastes that will impress your guests and elevate your cheese platter experience. Enjoy!

Chapter 18: Raspberry Sauces for Dressing Up Desserts

Raspberry sauces can transform ordinary desserts into decadent and visually stunning creations. In this chapter, we'll explore three delightful raspberry sauce recipes that are perfect for dressing up your favorite desserts.

Recipe 1: Raspberry Chocolate Fondant

Ingredients:

- 4 oz semisweet chocolate, chopped
- 1/2 cup unsalted butter
- 1/2 cup powdered sugar
- 2 large eggs
- 2 egg yolks
- 1/4 cup all-purpose flour
- 1/2 teaspoon vanilla extract
- Raspberry sauce (for filling and drizzling)
- Fresh raspberries for garnish
- Powdered sugar for dusting

Instructions:

1. Preheat Oven: Preheat your oven to 425°F (220°C). Grease and flour four ramekins or individual-sized baking dishes.
2. Melt Chocolate and Butter: In a microwave-safe bowl, melt the chopped semisweet chocolate and butter in 30-second intervals, stirring until smooth. Let it cool slightly.
3. Whisk Eggs and Sugar: In a separate bowl, whisk together the powdered sugar, eggs, egg yolks, and vanilla extract until well combined.
4. Combine Chocolate and Egg Mixtures: Gradually add the

melted chocolate mixture to the egg mixture, stirring until smooth.

5. Fold in Flour: Gently fold in the all-purpose flour until just combined.

6. Fill Ramekins: Divide the chocolate batter evenly among the prepared ramekins, filling each about halfway.

7. Add Raspberry Sauce: Place a teaspoon of raspberry sauce in the center of each batter-filled ramekin.

8. Cover with More Batter: Carefully spoon more chocolate batter over the raspberry sauce in each ramekin, covering it completely.

9. Bake: Bake in the preheated oven for 10-12 minutes, or until the edges are set but the center is still slightly jiggly.

10. Serve: Carefully run a knife around the edges of the fondants to loosen them, then invert each one onto a serving plate. Drizzle with more raspberry sauce, garnish with fresh raspberries, and dust with powdered sugar. Serve immediately while warm.

Recipe 2: Raspberry Sauce for Ice Cream Sundaes
Ingredients:

- Vanilla ice cream
- Fresh raspberries
- Chopped nuts (e.g., almonds or walnuts)
- Whipped cream
- Chocolate shavings (optional)
- Raspberry sauce

Instructions:

1. Assemble Ice Cream Sundaes: Scoop vanilla ice cream into serving bowls or glasses.
2. Add Fresh Raspberries: Scatter fresh raspberries over the ice cream.
3. Sprinkle Chopped Nuts: Sprinkle chopped nuts (e.g., almonds or walnuts) over the sundaes for crunch.
4. Top with Whipped Cream: Add a generous dollop of whipped cream on top.
5. Drizzle with Raspberry Sauce: Drizzle raspberry sauce over the sundaes, allowing it to cascade down the sides.
6. Garnish: Optionally, garnish with chocolate shavings for extra decadence.
7. Serve: Serve the raspberry sauce ice cream sundaes as a delightful and indulgent dessert.

Recipe 3: Raspberry Tiramisu
Ingredients:

- 1 1/2 cups heavy cream
- 1 cup mascarpone cheese
- 1/2 cup granulated sugar
- 1 teaspoon vanilla extract
- 1/2 cup strong brewed coffee, cooled
- 2 tablespoons coffee liqueur (optional)
- Ladyfingers
- Raspberry sauce
- Unsweetened cocoa powder for dusting

Instructions:

1. Prepare Mascarpone Mixture: In a mixing bowl, whip the heavy cream until stiff peaks form. In another bowl, whisk together the mascarpone cheese, granulated sugar, and vanilla extract until smooth. Gently fold the whipped cream into the mascarpone mixture until well combined.
2. Combine Coffee and Liqueur: In a shallow dish, combine the cooled strong brewed coffee and coffee liqueur (if using).
3. Assemble Tiramisu: Dip ladyfingers into the coffee mixture and arrange them in the bottom of a serving dish or individual dessert cups.
4. Add Mascarpone Mixture: Spread a layer of the mascarpone mixture over the soaked ladyfingers.
5. Drizzle with Raspberry Sauce: Drizzle raspberry sauce over the mascarpone layer.
6. Repeat Layers: Continue layering with soaked ladyfingers, mascarpone mixture, and raspberry sauce until you reach the top of the serving dish.
7. Chill: Cover and refrigerate the raspberry tiramisu for at least 4

hours or overnight to allow the flavors to meld.

8. Dust with Cocoa: Before serving, dust the top with unsweetened cocoa powder.
9. Serve: Serve the raspberry tiramisu as a luscious and fruity twist on the classic Italian dessert.

These raspberry sauce recipes for dressing up desserts will add a touch of elegance and flavor to your sweet creations. Whether it's a decadent chocolate fondant, a luscious ice cream sundae, or a fruity tiramisu, these recipes are perfect for indulgent occasions or simply satisfying your dessert cravings. Enjoy!

Chapter 19: Raspberry Sauces for the Holidays

Raspberry sauces can bring a festive touch to your holiday celebrations, whether you're enjoying Thanksgiving, Christmas, or New Year's. In this chapter, we'll explore three delightful raspberry sauce recipes that are perfect for holiday occasions.

Recipe 1: Raspberry Cranberry Sauce for Thanksgiving
Ingredients:

- 12 oz fresh cranberries
- 1 cup granulated sugar
- 1/2 cup water
- 1/2 cup raspberry sauce
- Zest and juice of 1 orange
- 1 cinnamon stick
- Pinch of salt

Instructions:

1. Combine Ingredients: In a saucepan, combine the fresh cranberries, granulated sugar, water, raspberry sauce, orange zest, orange juice, cinnamon stick, and a pinch of salt.
2. Cook: Place the saucepan over medium heat and bring the mixture to a simmer. Reduce the heat to low and let it cook, stirring occasionally, for about 15-20 minutes, or until the cranberries burst and the sauce thickens.
3. Cool: Remove the cinnamon stick and let the raspberry cranberry sauce cool to room temperature.
4. Serve: Transfer the sauce to a serving bowl and serve as a delightful and tangy accompaniment to your Thanksgiving turkey and holiday spread.

Recipe 2: Raspberry Linzer Cookies for Christmas
Ingredients:
For the Cookies:

- 1 cup unsalted butter, softened
- 1/2 cup granulated sugar
- 1 large egg
- 1 teaspoon vanilla extract
- 2 1/2 cups all-purpose flour
- 1/2 teaspoon ground cinnamon
- 1/4 teaspoon salt
- Raspberry sauce (for filling)
- Powdered sugar (for dusting)

For the Raspberry Filling:

- 1/2 cup raspberry sauce
- 1/4 cup raspberry jam

Instructions:
For the Cookies:

1. Cream Butter and Sugar: In a mixing bowl, cream together the softened unsalted butter and granulated sugar until light and fluffy.
2. Add Egg and Vanilla: Beat in the egg and vanilla extract.
3. Mix Dry Ingredients: In a separate bowl, whisk together the all-purpose flour, ground cinnamon, and salt.
4. Combine Wet and Dry Ingredients: Gradually add the dry ingredients to the butter mixture, mixing until a dough forms.
5. Chill Dough: Divide the dough into two portions, flatten them into discs, wrap in plastic wrap, and chill in the refrigerator for at least 30 minutes.
6. Roll Out Dough: Preheat your oven to 350°F (175°C). Roll out one disc of dough on a floured surface to about 1/4-inch thickness.
7. Cut Shapes: Using Linzer cookie cutters, cut out an even number of solid and cutout cookies.
8. Bake: Place the cookies on a parchment paper-lined baking sheet and bake for 10-12 minutes, or until the edges are lightly golden. Let them cool on the baking sheet for a few minutes before transferring to a wire rack to cool completely.

For the Raspberry Filling:

1. Prepare Raspberry Filling: In a bowl, mix together the raspberry sauce and raspberry jam until smooth.
2. Assemble Cookies: Spread raspberry filling on the solid cookies, leaving a small border around the edges. Top with cutout cookies to create cookie sandwiches.
3. Dust with Powdered Sugar: Dust the tops of the cookies with powdered sugar using a fine-mesh sieve.

4. Serve: Serve the raspberry Linzer cookies as festive and delightful treats for your Christmas celebrations.

Recipe 3: New Year's Raspberry Champagne Punch
Ingredients:

- 1 bottle of champagne or sparkling wine, chilled
- 1/2 cup raspberry sauce
- 1/4 cup orange liqueur (e.g., Grand Marnier)
- 1/4 cup fresh orange juice
- Fresh raspberries and orange slices for garnish
- Ice cubes (optional)

Instructions:

1. Mix Ingredients: In a large pitcher, combine the chilled champagne or sparkling wine, raspberry sauce, orange liqueur, and fresh orange juice. Stir gently to mix.
2. Chill: If desired, chill the mixture in the refrigerator for about 30 minutes to allow the flavors to meld.
3. Serve: Pour the raspberry champagne punch into glasses filled with ice cubes (if using). Garnish with fresh raspberries and orange slices.
4. Toast: Raise your glasses and toast to the New Year with this sparkling and fruity raspberry champagne punch.

These raspberry sauce recipes for the holidays are perfect for adding a touch of sweetness and festivity to your special occasions. Whether you're celebrating Thanksgiving with cranberry sauce, baking Christmas cookies, or ringing in the New Year with a sparkling punch, these recipes will help make your holidays even more memorable. Enjoy!

Chapter 20: Raspberry Sauce as Edible Gifts

Raspberry sauces make delightful and personalized edible gifts for friends and family. In this chapter, we'll explore creative ways to share the joy of homemade raspberry sauce with others, including gift jars, gift basket ideas, and homemade labels and packaging.

Recipe 1: Raspberry Sauce Jars

Ingredients:

- Raspberry sauce (see your favorite raspberry sauce recipe from earlier chapters)
- Small glass jars with lids
- Ribbon or twine for decoration
- Gift tags with instructions (optional)

Instructions:

1. Prepare Raspberry Sauce: Prepare a batch of your favorite raspberry sauce recipe from earlier chapters.
2. Cool: Allow the raspberry sauce to cool to room temperature.
3. Fill Jars: Carefully pour the raspberry sauce into small glass jars with lids. Leave a little space at the top for expansion.
4. Seal Jars: Seal the jars with their lids.
5. Decorate: Decorate the jars with ribbon or twine to make them visually appealing.
6. Add Gift Tags: Optionally, attach gift tags with instructions for using the raspberry sauce. Include suggestions for pairing it with desserts, breakfasts, or other dishes.
7. Present: Present the raspberry sauce jars as thoughtful and delicious gifts for any occasion. They're perfect for birthdays, anniversaries, or just to show appreciation.

Recipe 2: Raspberry Sauce Gift Basket Ideas
Ingredients:

- Raspberry sauce jars (prepared as described above)
- Assorted desserts (e.g., cookies, brownies, or cakes)
- Fresh raspberries
- Whipped cream
- Small kitchen tools or utensils (e.g., mini spatulas, dessert spoons)
- Cellophane or gift wrap
- Basket or gift box
- Ribbon or bow

Instructions:

1. Select Desserts: Choose an assortment of desserts that pair well with raspberry sauce. Consider homemade treats or high-quality store-bought options.
2. Assemble Basket or Gift Box: Line a basket or gift box with cellophane or gift wrap to create a festive base.
3. Arrange Items: Place the raspberry sauce jars, assorted desserts, fresh raspberries, and small kitchen tools or utensils (if desired) in the basket or gift box. Arrange them attractively.
4. Decorate: Add a ribbon or bow to the outside of the basket or gift box to make it visually appealing.
5. Include a Note: Don't forget to include a handwritten note or card with a personalized message.
6. Present: Present the raspberry sauce gift basket to your recipient. It's a thoughtful and delicious gift that's sure to be appreciated.

Recipe 3: Homemade Raspberry Sauce Labels and Packaging
Ingredients:

- Raspberry sauce (see your favorite raspberry sauce recipe)
- Printable labels
- Colored paper or cardstock
- Scissors or a paper cutter
- Glue or adhesive tape
- Ribbon or twine (optional)

Instructions:

1. Prepare Raspberry Sauce: Prepare a batch of your homemade raspberry sauce as desired.
2. Design Labels: Create or download printable labels for your raspberry sauce. You can use graphic design software or find templates online. Customize the labels with the sauce's name, ingredients, and any other information you'd like to include.
3. Print Labels: Print the labels on colored paper or cardstock.
4. Cut Labels: Use scissors or a paper cutter to cut out the labels into the desired shape and size.
5. Attach Labels: Use glue or adhesive tape to attach the labels to the jars or containers of raspberry sauce.
6. Decorate Packaging: If desired, decorate the packaging with ribbon or twine for an extra special touch.
7. Present: Present the beautifully labeled raspberry sauce jars as homemade gifts. They not only taste delicious but also showcase your creativity and thoughtfulness.

These ideas for using raspberry sauce as edible gifts allow you to share your love for homemade treats with others. Whether you choose to give jars of raspberry sauce, assemble gift baskets, or create custom labels and packaging, your recipients will appreciate the effort and the delicious gift from your kitchen. Enjoy spreading joy with these raspberry sauce gift ideas!

In conclusion, the "Raspberry Sauce Cookbook" has taken you on a flavorful journey through the world of raspberry sauces, offering a wide range of delicious recipes for various occasions. From breakfast delights to savory dishes, sweet treats, and even festive edible gifts, raspberries have shown their versatility and unique ability to enhance a multitude of culinary experiences.

This cookbook has provided you with a comprehensive collection of raspberry sauce recipes, each designed to delight your taste buds and inspire your culinary creativity. Whether you're a seasoned chef or a beginner in the kitchen, these recipes offer something for everyone to enjoy.

Raspberry sauce has proven to be a versatile ingredient, capable of adding a burst of sweet and tangy flavor to a wide array of dishes. From the classic raspberry coulis to exotic international flavors, and from indulgent desserts to healthy eating options, raspberries have shined as a star ingredient throughout this cookbook.

Additionally, we explored ways to share the joy of homemade raspberry sauce with others, whether as thoughtful gifts or as a way to elevate your holiday celebrations. The creative ideas for gift jars, gift baskets, and personalized labels and packaging have shown that raspberry sauce can be a heartfelt and delicious present for loved ones.

As you continue your culinary adventures, don't hesitate to experiment with these raspberry sauce recipes, adapt them to your preferences, and create your own mouthwatering dishes. Whether you're cooking for yourself or sharing with others, the delightful flavors of raspberries are sure to bring joy to every meal.

Thank you for joining us on this culinary journey through the "Raspberry Sauce Cookbook." May your kitchen be filled with the sweet aroma and vibrant taste of raspberries as you explore the endless possibilities they offer. Enjoy your cooking and the delicious raspberry creations that await!